The Quarrel

Thelma Page

Illustrated by Jacqui Thomas

OXFORD
UNIVERSITY PRESS

OXFORD
UNIVERSITY PRESS

Great Clarendon Street, Oxford OX2 6DP

Oxford University Press is a department of the University of Oxford.
It furthers the University's objective of excellence in research, scholarship,
and education by publishing worldwide in

Oxford New York

Auckland Bangkok Buenos Aires Cape Town Chennai
Dar es Salaam Delhi Hong Kong Istanbul Karachi Kolkata
Kuala Lumpur Madrid Melbourne Mexico City Mumbai Nairobi
São Paulo Shanghai Singapore Taipei Tokyo Toronto

First published 2002

British Library Cataloguing in Publication Data

Data available

ISBN 0 19 919503 X

1 3 5 7 9 10 8 6 4 2

Printed in Hong Kong

1

Vicky and Rachel had known each other for a long time. They had started school on the same day and had birthdays in the same week. Their last names, Martin and Miller, were even next to each other on the class register.

Most of the time they were good friends but today something had happened.

Vicky was having a bad day. When everyone came in from play, she stayed in the cloakroom, her face in her hands.

'What's the matter, Vicky, are you hurt?' asked Mrs Kumar.

Vicky wouldn't say.

‘Rachel,’ said Mrs Kumar, ‘do you know why Vicky is upset?’

Rachel wouldn’t say anything either. Vicky came and sat down, but kept away from Rachel.

'Well, let's get on then,' said Mrs Kumar. 'I've been asked to tell you about this painting competition.'

She held up a poster.

'The painting has to be something to do with "The Sea",' went on Mrs Kumar. 'All the schools in the area have been asked to send in pictures.'

'Can older children enter as well?' asked Rachel. 'My brother is much better at painting than I am.'

'There are different age groups,' explained Mrs Kumar. 'Your paintings would be in the five to seven group. Your brother would be in the eight to elevens, so don't worry about the older children winning everything.'

Mrs Kumar looked at Vicky, hoping it might cheer her up. Vicky was good at drawing and painting. But she was still looking down at the floor, with her face in her hands.

'What's the prize?' asked Michael.

'Free tickets to the pantomime, and a chance to meet the stars afterwards,' said Mrs Kumar.

She showed them the poster. It showed an old-fashioned sailing ship with Dick Whittington and his cat. The ship had sailors climbing the rigging. Around the edge of the poster there were photographs of the main actors in the pantomime.

'You could paint a ship like the one on the poster; or a stormy sea; or a sunny beach. It can be a real place or an imaginary one. There will be time for all of you to do a painting in school this week, so start thinking of some ideas.'

'Look, Zara's in the pantomime. Just imagine talking to a real pop star. I'd ask for her autograph,' Rachel said excitedly.

Everyone began to look interested. Zara was a famous singer with a pop band.

'Vicky, would you like to start a painting?' asked Mrs Kumar. Vicky got up miserably and went to get her overall. Other arms shot up.

'Can I paint, pleeease?' called out Robert.

Mrs Kumar laughed. 'All right. Robert, Michael and Rachel, go and join Vicky. Everyone else, I'd like you to finish the stories we started yesterday.'

'I'm going to paint "Jaws",' decided Robert. 'I'll put some men in a little boat over here and a great shark with a wide-open mouth coming up out of the water.'

'That's a good idea,' said Rachel. 'I'm going to do a shark too.'

'You can't, that's copying,' objected Robert, putting his hand up. 'Mrs Kumar, it's not fair! I'm painting "Jaws" and Rachel is copying my idea.'

'All right, I'll paint a killer whale,' said Rachel. 'I'll paint the whale I saw in a film. The whale is trapped in a pool but he jumps over a wall and gets to the open sea.'

'I'll draw a boat in a storm with lightning and massive waves,' said Michael. 'What are you doing, Vicky?'

Vicky didn't answer. She was quietly washing thin blue paint across her whole page. As it dried she picked up a very fine brush and painted wavy fronds of seaweed.

Then she put tiny sea horses and brightly patterned tropical fish among the seaweed. She added starfish and stripy shells, and in one corner she painted a mermaid with long flowing hair.

Rachel had painted a huge black and white whale. Now she needed to clean the black paint out of her brush, so she went to get fresh water. As she came back she tripped.

Her beaker of water spilled over Vicky's painting.

'Oh Vicky, I am so sorry,' she gasped. 'I really didn't mean it. It was an accident.'

For a second Vicky looked up at Rachel, then she burst into tears.

Mrs Kumar came over. ‘Oh dear, what a shame. Vicky, that was a lovely painting. Don’t worry. I’m sure we can rescue it. Luckily it was clean water.’

Mrs Kumar fetched some paper towels and gently dried up most of the water. ‘Look, I think if we leave it to dry now it will be all right.’

Vicky didn't care. She went to the book corner, still in tears. Mrs Kumar brought tissues to dry her cheeks. Vicky's face was red and hot, but it wasn't just the tears. Mrs Kumar had noticed something.

'Rachel,' she said. 'Will you go to the office and ask Mrs Carter if she can come here, please?'

Mrs Carter came back with Rachel. She bent down beside Vicky and felt her forehead.

'She is very hot,' she said. 'I'll phone her mother straight away. Come on, Vicky, you come and sit with me for a bit.'

‘What did I do? What is it?’ asked Rachel, really worried.

‘I think Vicky might have chicken pox,’ replied Mrs Kumar. ‘She’s very hot and she’s got a few spots on her face and neck. When you are ill it makes you feel a bit weepy and fed up. I expect the doctor will give her some medicine to cool her down. Then she will need to rest for a bit. She’ll soon be better.’

Then it was Rachel's turn to be upset. 'I've been horrible,' she admitted. 'At playtime I saw the spots on Vicky's face. I thought she looked funny so I told Tom. We called her "Spotty Vick". That was why she was upset after playtime. It was just a joke. We didn't mean to be unkind.'

'Well, whether you meant it or not, it was an unkind thing to do,' said Mrs Kumar. 'No one likes being called names. You know that, don't you?'

Rachel nodded. 'I'm really sorry. And I didn't mean to spoil her painting, I just tripped.'

'Poor Vicky. She has had a bad day. I think the best thing you can do is to write a little note to Vicky to say that you are sorry.'

2

Rachel missed Vicky. She seemed to be away for ages. Then one morning Vicky's mum came in. She had a quick word with Mrs Kumar. 'The doctor says Vicky is well enough to come back to school, but she's a bit worried. There are a few red marks where the spots have healed and Vicky thinks that someone might tease her.'

‘I’ll make sure they don’t,’ said Rachel. ‘I will make sure nobody says anything. I think we should have a new class rule, “No name-calling allowed”.’

Mrs Kumar smiled, ‘That sounds like a good idea,’ she said. ‘We’ll talk about it later. Now it’s time to go into Assembly.’

3

They had a story, a prayer and learned to sing a new song. Then Mrs Archer, the head teacher, picked up a large package.

'Now I have something very special to tell you,' said Mrs Archer. 'Vicky Martin, can you come up here, please?'

Vicky got up, wondering what it could be about. Everyone was looking at her and she went red. She went to the front of the hall.

'I am sure you all remember painting a picture for a competition,' said Mrs Archer. 'Lots of schools entered and they have just chosen the winner. Vicky, congratulations! Your painting has won first prize. Would you like to open this package?'

Vicky undid the sticky tape and tore off the paper. It was her painting inside a proper frame.

'The judges said they especially liked the watery effect of your painting,' went on Mrs Archer. 'Look, everyone. Vicky decided to paint an underwater scene. I like all the tiny fishes and the mermaid over here in the corner.'

Mrs Archer pointed out details in the painting as she spoke. 'Vicky chose lovely colours and put in a lot of sea creatures. She painted everything very carefully.'

Everyone clapped and clapped.

'Do you mind if we hang it here in the hall for the rest of the day, Vicky?' said Mrs Archer. 'Then you can take it home at home time. And here is your prize, tickets for the pantomime in town. Well done!'

Everyone clapped again.

4

At home, that evening, Vicky opened the envelope. There were pantomime tickets for two children and two adults.

'Who shall we take with us, Vicky?' asked her mum.

'I want to take Rachel,' said Vicky.

'Oh, I hoped you might say that, said Vicky's mum. 'Are you two friends again?'

'Yes,' answered Vicky, 'and without Rachel I may not have won the prize.'

'What do you mean?' asked Vicky's mum.

‘Well, when Rachel tripped and spilled the water on my picture, I thought she had ruined it. But when it dried it gave the painting a watery look,’ explained Vicky, ‘and that was what the judges liked most about it. So it’s only fair that Rachel shares the prize, isn’t it?’